W9-CLW-257

ACID RAIN

Sally Morgan

SEA-TO-SEA
Mankato Collingwood London

This edition first published in 2010 by
Sea-to-Sea Publications
Distributed by Black Rabbit Books
P.O. Box 3263, Mankato, Minnesota 56002

Printed in USA

Library of Congress Cataloging-in-Publication Data

Morgan, Sally.
  Acid rain / Sally Morgan.
      p. cm. -- (Earth SOS)
  Includes index.
  ISBN 978-1-59771-221-7 (hardcover)
  1. Acid rain--Environmental aspects--Juvenile literature. I. Title.
  TD195.44.M673 2010
  363.738'6--dc22
                                2008053157

9 8 7 6 5 4 3 2

Published by arrangement with the Watts
Publishing Group Ltd., London.

EARTH SOS is based on the series EarthWatch published by Franklin Watts.
It was produced for Franklin Watts by Bender Richardson White,
P O Box 266, Uxbridge UB9 5NX.
Project Editor: Lionel Bender
Text Editor: Jenny Vaughan
Original text adapted and updated by: Jenny Vaughan
Designer: Ben White
Picture Researchers: Cathy Stastny and Daniela Marceddu
Media Conversion and Make-up: Mike Weintroub, MW Graphics,
and Clare Oliver
Production: Kim Richardson

Picture Credits Ecoscene: cover main photo (Sally Morgan), and pages 1
(Sally Morgan), 5 top (Angela Hampton), 9 top (Winkley), 16, 17 bottom
(Meissner), 19 bottom (Anthony Cooper), 20 (Andrew Brown), 23 top
(Anthony Cooper), 28 (Ian Harwood). Environmental Images: pages 11
bottom (Matt Sampson), 24 (Leslie Garland), 25 top (Martin Bond), 25
bottom (Daniel Beltra). Oxford Scientific Films: cover small photo (Niall
Benvie) and pages 5 bottom (Mike Slater), 6 (Kathie Atkinson), 7 (Carson
Baldwin Jr.), 9 bottom (Michael Leach), 14 (David Cayless), 15 top (G. I.
Bernard), 19 top (Lena Beyer), 20 top (Barrie E. Watts), 22 (Survival
Anglia/John Harris), 23 bottom (Marty Cordano), 26 (Okapia/Kjell-Arne
Larsson), 27 top (Okapia). Panos Pictures: pages 11 top (J. Holmes).
Planet Earth Pictures: page 27 bottom (Norbert Wu). Science Photo
Library, London: pages 4–5 (Simon Fraser), 8–9 (John Mead), 17 top
(Martin Bond), 21 bottom (Simon Fraser), 29 top (Astrid & Hanns-Frieder
Michler). The Stockmarket Photo Agency, Inc.: cover globe image and
pages 12, 15 bottom, 18, 29 bottom.

Artwork by Raymond Turvey

Note to parents and teachers: Every effort has been made by the publisher to ensure that websites listed are suitable for children, that they are of the highest educational value, and that they contain no inappropriate or offensive material. However, because of the nature of the Internet, it is impossible to guarantee that the contents of these sites will not be altered. We strongly advise that Internet access is supervised by a responsible adult.

CONTENTS

THE PROBLEM

Acid rain is a kind of pollution. It damages buildings. It also kills trees, and harms wildlife in lakes and rivers.

Acid rain has killed the trees on this hillside.

Polluting the rain

Factories, cars, and power plants burn fuel. This releases gases into the air. These gases mix with rain, and pollute it. **Pollution** is the name we give to harmful substances in our environment.

What is acid rain?

Acids are liquids that can wear away metals and stone. Gases from burning fuels mix with rain. This makes a weak acid. This is called acid rain.

Dipping in a pond helps find out whether acid rain is damaging the plants and animals that live in the water.

Nothing new

Acid rain has been around for about 200 years. It first formed when people started burning a lot of coal. It also forms when we burn oil and natural gas. We call these kinds of fuels **fossil fuels**. When they burn, they give off gases that cause acid rain.

Acid rain has damaged this statue in Italy.

THE WATER CYCLE

Two-thirds of the Earth is covered by water. This is mostly salty seawater. A small amount is fresh water. Rivers and most lakes contain fresh water.

Rainwater fills rivers and streams. These flow into oceans.

Changing water

When water is very cold, it becomes solid ice. As ice gets warmer, it becomes liquid water. When liquid water gets warm, it becomes a gas called **water vapor**. We say it has **evaporated**.

How rain forms

Water in oceans, lakes, and on land evaporates as the Sun heats it. It rises into the sky, cools, and becomes liquid again. We say it has **condensed**. It falls as rain.

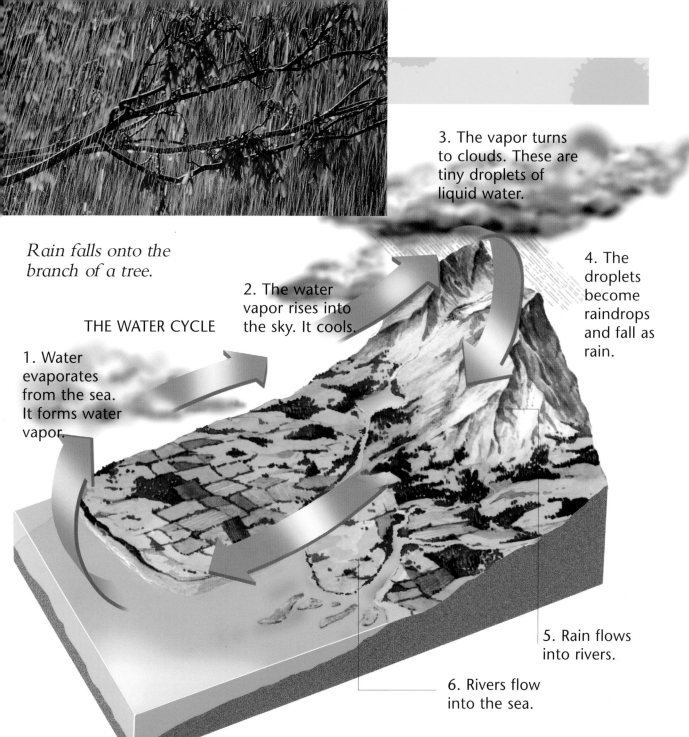

Rain falls onto the branch of a tree.

THE WATER CYCLE

3. The vapor turns to clouds. These are tiny droplets of liquid water.

4. The droplets become raindrops and fall as rain.

2. The water vapor rises into the sky. It cools.

1. Water evaporates from the sea. It forms water vapor.

5. Rain flows into rivers.

6. Rivers flow into the sea.

Try this

Breathe onto a window pane on a cold day. A cloud of tiny water drops forms. Water vapor in your breath has condensed to form liquid water.

Back to the oceans

Rainwater flows into rivers and the oceans. It evaporates, and becomes clouds again. We call this endless process the water cycle.

ACIDS AND ALKALIS

Acids taste sour, like lemon juice. Alkalis are the opposite of acids. Alkalis taste bitter. Soap is an alkali.

Gases from burnt fuel mix with water in clouds. They form acid rain.

Acids

We measure how strong an acid is by using units called **pH**. Anything that measures between 1 and 6 is an acid. Weaker acids have higher numbers. So, for example, apple juice has a pH of about 5. But some very strong acids, which are used by scientists and in industry, may have a pH of 1 or 2.

Eco Thought
Some acid rain has a pH of around 2.4. That is almost the same as lemon juice.

Alkalis

We also measure **alkalis** in pH units. Anything with a pH between 8 and 14 is an alkali. Soap has a pH of about 9.

Neutral substances

Some liquids, such as pure water, are **neutral**. Neutral substances have a pH of 7. We can turn an acid into a neutral substance by adding an alkali to it.

Natural hot springs like this can give off gases that make acid rain.

Acid in ponds can harm living things.

9

ACID RAIN FORMS

All rain is slightly acid. There is a gas called carbon dioxide in the air. It mixes with rain, to make a pH of around 6. Acid rain can have a pH of 4.

Causes of acid rain

One main gas that causes acid rain is **sulfur dioxide**. Some comes from volcanoes, hot springs, and other natural sources. But most comes from burning fuel. Other acid rain gases are **nitrogen oxides**. These also come from burning fuels.

POLLUTED AIR
AND ACID RAIN

- Sources of pollution
- Some acid rain
- Serious acid rain

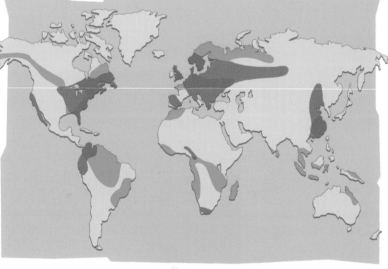

From gas to acid

When coal, oil, and gas burn, they produce a substance called sulfur. When sulfur burns, it makes a gas called sulfur dioxide. If this mixes with water, it forms sulfuric acid. Many substances also produce **carbon dioxide** gas. This forms carbonic acid.

Eco Thought
One-seventh of coal is sulfur. Gas contains much less. So burning coal causes far more acid rain than burning gas.

As cars burn gasoline, nitrogen oxides are let out. This gas causes acid rain.

On the Ground

Pollution can help form the gas **ozone**. This filters harmful sunlight. But it can harm living things, too.

Burning fuels

We make our electricity in power plants. Often, these burn fuels such as coal, oil, or gas. Cars burn gasoline, which is made from oil. All these send waste gases into the air, causing acid rain.

Sunlight

Sunlight helps the harmful gases mix with water vapor. This mixing forms acid rain.

*This dirty mist is called **smog**. It is a mix of polluting gases.*

SPREAD BY WIND

When the wind is close to the ground, trees and buildings slow it down. High in the sky, it can blow much faster.

High chimneys

Factories used to have short chimneys. These spread pollution to the ground nearby. Starting about 150 years ago, people built tall chimneys. These send pollution high into the sky. There, it forms acid rain. Strong winds carry pollution for long distances.

Air pollution from a factory in Scotland.

THE ACID RAIN CYCLE

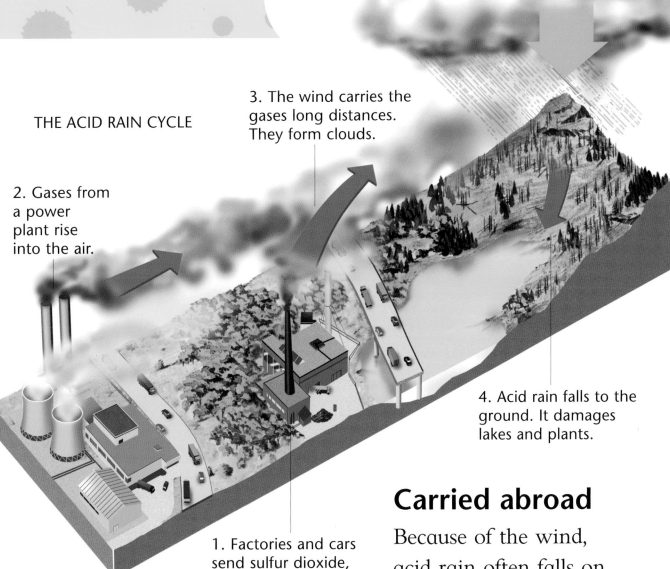

2. Gases from a power plant rise into the air.

3. The wind carries the gases long distances. They form clouds.

4. Acid rain falls to the ground. It damages lakes and plants.

1. Factories and cars send sulfur dioxide, nitrogen oxides, and other harmful gases into the air.

Carried abroad

Because of the wind, acid rain often falls on countries that did not cause it. For example, nearly all the acid rain in Norway comes from other countries. Canada gets acid rain from the US. Countries must work together to solve this problem.

Try this

Which way does the wind blow in your area? Look at a map to see where your local power plant is. Where does the pollution go?

SOIL AND WATER

When acid rain falls to the ground, it makes the soil acid. It runs into rivers and lakes, and makes them acid, too.

When fresh water like this lake gets too acid, it harms the plants and animals in it.

Acid rain

Some soil, such as chalky soil, has alkali in it. We say it is alkaline. Acid rain makes it neutral, and does not harm it much. Some soils are already acid, especially if there are pine trees. Pine leaves make the soil acid. Acid rain makes this worse.

On the Ground

A lake in the Adirondack Mountains in New York state has a pH of 4.2. This is too acid for fish to live in.

14

Acid soil

There are chemicals in the soil that plants need. We call these **nutrients**. Plants draw these up through their roots. Acid rain can wash nutrients away, so the plants are harmed. Acid rain puts poisons into the soil. These get into plants, and wash into rivers and lakes.

Plants' roots take up water and nutrients from the soil. Plants need these to live, grow, and stay healthy.

Scientists measure the pH of water in a lake. They want to see if it has been harmed by acid rain.

DYING TREES

Acid rain affects all plants. Trees suffer the worst. Conifers, such as pine and fir trees, are most damaged by acid rain.

These trees in Hungary have lost their leaves because of acid rain.

Falling leaves

Trees take up poisons from acid rain in the soil. These make their leaves fall off. A tree needs its leaves to make food from sunlight.

Eco Thought

In Norway, the damage that acid rain does to the environment costs around $450 million every year!

16

Rotting roots

If trees lose too many leaves, they cannot make enough food. Branches die, and then whole trees die. But this can be balanced. If rotting roots and branches are left in the soil, they make alkalis. These reduce the acid.

These trees are protected from acid rain, to see if they grow better than trees outside.

Try this

Plant garden cress seeds in two trays. When they start to grow, water one tray with lemon juice. Water the other with rainwater. What happens?

Acid rain has harmed these leaves. It has made them turn brown.

DYING LAKES

Acid rain flows into lakes. The water in the lakes becomes acid, too.

Eggs and acid rain

The first animals to be harmed by acid in lake water are water animals. Acid damages the eggs of fish, frogs, toads, and newts. As a result, they may not hatch, so there are fewer young.

On the Ground
Acid lake water is blue. Healthy water is murky, because of tiny living things in it.

This lake is in Germany. The plants and animals in it have died, because of acid rain.

Poison in the water

Some water animals, such as shrimp, have hard, outer shells. Acid eats these away. The animals die. On land, soil contains the metal aluminum. Acid rain washes this into rivers and lakes. It is poison and kills fish, especially some kinds of trout and salmon.

Food chains

The living things in a lake need each other. For example, fish eat shrimp, and herons eat fish. So, if the shrimps die, so will the fish and then the herons.

This water lily is growing in water with an acid level of pH 4.8. Few plants can live in this.

Acid rain damages frogs' eggs and kills the flies that frogs eat. This means there are fewer frogs in the world.

Eco Thought

In Sweden, 4,000 lakes are too acid for fish to live in them.

DAMAGED STONE

Ordinary rain damages some kinds of stone. Acid rain does even more damage.

Attacking stone

Many buildings are made from **limestone** and sandstone. These kinds of stone are easy to cut and carve. But acid rain easily wears these away, and spoils the carvings. This is called **erosion**. The stone also starts to look black and dirty.

Natural rainwater has worn away these rocks in the USA.

Saving stone

We cannot easily repair damage to stone. But there is a special substance we can paint over the stone, to protect it. Acid rain also damages plastic, glass, and metal. Acid in the air can even damage paintings in galleries. Special air conditioning can help stop this.

Plants called lichens grow on rocks, walls, and trees. They are some of the first living things that acid rain kills.

Try this

Find a piece of chalk or limestone. Put some drops of vinegar on it. The vinegar attacks the stone. It gives off carbon dioxide gas.

Acid rain has damaged this building in Poland. It will be hard to repair.

Eco Thought

Some buildings and statues in Greece are 2,500 years old. Acid rain has been damaging them.

AIR POLLUTION

Acid rain looks like ordinary rain. But the gases that cause it are full of pollution. This air is bad for our health.

We can see the pollution in the air over some cities.

Breathing in polluted air

Gases like nitrogen oxides and sulfur dioxide harm our lungs. This is bad for people who have breathing problems, such as **asthma**.

This woman has asthma. Her inhaler helps her to breathe.

Eco Thought

In 1952, there was thick smog over London, in England. It was caused by smoke from coal fires. It killed thousands of people.

City air and trees

In cities, there is a lot of pollution in the air. It comes from cars, factories, and power plants. This polluted air is very bad for our health. It makes a dirty fog, called smog. It is worst on sunny days. But some kinds of trees are very good at living in polluted air. Their leaves can take some poison gases from the air. Plane trees collect the poisons from the air in their bark. The bark peels off, and the tree stays healthy.

This man is using a machine to measure the amount of pollution in the air. If it is high, people can be warned about it.

CUTTING POLLUTION

To stop acid rain, we must put less pollution into the air. This is difficult, because there are so many cars. These add nitrogen oxides to the air.

Cutting back

Many countries now have laws to stop factories and power plants from putting polluting gases into the air. Power plants and factories often have filters on their chimneys. These get rid of gases.

Try this
Try to find out about your local power plant. Does the fuel it uses pollute the air?

This new power plant has a filter on its chimney to stop pollution from getting into the air.

Clean energy

Some power plants make electricity using energy from the Sun, water, or the wind. These do not pollute the air.

Cleaner cars

New cars have **catalytic converters** attached to their **exhaust pipes**. These stop harmful gases from getting into the air.

*Water flows through this dam. It works **turbines**, which are machines that make electricity.*

These are wind turbines. As they turn in the wind, they make electricity.

FIGHTING THE ACID

In many countries, people are working hard to get rid of the acid that has built up in the soil and water.

This helicopter is dropping lime, to help reduce acid in the soil.

Treating the soil

When soil is too acid, farmers put a substance called lime on it. Lime is an alkali. It neutralizes the soil, which means it makes it balanced. Lime is also added to lakes, to stop them from getting too acid. Lime has to be added often, to undo the effects of acid rain.

Try this

Some water from lakes and rivers is too acid for us to use in our homes. Find out if this true in your area.

This scientist is testing water to see if it is clean and not too acid.

On the Ground

Since 1990, the US government has been trying to get factories to create less acid rain. This has helped to save many forests.

Lime for fish

In Norway, some lakes and rivers were too acid for fish and other water animals to live. Now, lime is added every year. Water animals and fish such as trout can survive in this water, and stay healthy.

Lime in acid water helps trout to live in it.

WHAT CAN WE DO?

Look at trees and buildings in your area. Can you see any damage that has been caused by acid rain?

These children are checking trees, to see if acid rain has damaged them.

Look for damage

Look for damage to trees, such as yellow leaves and dead branches. The best time to do this is in early summer. Birch, beech, and conifer trees are often the most harmed. When their leaves are damaged, trees become weak, and may die.

Try this

Acid rain makes holes and cracks in buildings. Statues lose their eyes and noses. Look at buildings and statues in your area. Has acid rain damaged them?

Get active

We can cut down on pollution, to help stop acid rain. We can walk or cycle instead of going by car. We can save energy, so that power plants send out less pollution. For example, we can turn off lights and machines, such as computers, when we are not using them.

A catalytic converter helps stop air pollution.

On the Ground

In many countries, there are rules that say people must not drive cars or trucks that send out a lot of pollution.

This man is testing a car engine, to see how much pollution it is making.

29

FACT FILE

Caves

Rain is often slightly acid, even when there is no pollution. This acid rain soaks into cracks in rocks and carves out caves under the ground.

Cars

There are now more than 700 million cars, trucks, and other vehicles on the world's roads. This is more than 10 times the number in 1950.

More acid

Rain in Europe is 70 times more acid today than in 1950.

Sweden

Between 1970 and 1988, Sweden cut the amount of sulfur dioxide it put into the air by three-quarters.

Green hair

Acid rain can turn hair green! Acid in drinking water attacks the metal in old water pipes. The metal gets into the water. It can make us ill, and change our hair color.

Problem areas

Acid rain has done most damage in northern Europe, North America, Russia, Mexico, Australia, Japan, and China.

Filters

There are filters we can use on car exhaust pipes and factory chimneys. Scientists believe these will cut the amount of sulfur dioxide made in Europe by four-fifths.

Websites

www.epa.gov/acidrain/education/site_kids/index.htm

www.ec.gc.ca/acidrain/kids.html

GLOSSARY

Acid A substance with a pH of less than 7. There are weak acids, such as lemon juice or vinegar, and strong ones that are dangerous and can burn.

Alkali The opposite of acid. An alkali has a pH of more than 7. Soap and baking powder are alkalis.

Asthma A problem some people have with their lungs, which means they find it hard to breathe.

Carbon dioxide One of the gases in the air. When we breathe, we take in a gas called oxygen, and breathe out carbon dioxide. It can mix with water to make a very weak acid.

Catalytic converter A device that reduces harmful exhaust fumes given out by cars.

Condense To change from a gas to a liquid.

Erosion Wearing away the natural surface of something.

Evaporate To change from a liquid to a gas.

Exhaust pipe A pipe at the back of a car. Waste fumes come out of it when the engine is running.

Fossil fuels Fuels such as coal and oil. They formed from the bodies of plants and animals that died millions of years ago.

Limestone A kind of rock. Lime is made by heating limestone.

Neutral Something that is neither acid nor alkali is neutral. It has a pH of 7.

Nitrogen oxide A kind of gas that can form acid rain.

Nutrients Substances living things need to help them grow.

Ozone A kind of gas found high up in the air.

pH The unit we use to measure how acid something is. Anything with a pH below 7 is acid. If something has a pH above 7, it is an alkali. The highest number is 14, which is a very strong alkali.

Pollution Dirty substances that damage the environment.

Smog A kind of dirty fog. It is caused by pollution from factories and cars.

Sulfur dioxide A kind of gas that forms acid rain.

Turbine A motor with a set of blades. These are turned by moving gas or liquid.

Water vapor Water in the form of a gas. If liquid water is warmed, it turns into water vapor.

INDEX